Peaceful Productivity
Mindful Time Management Strategies

Table of Contents

Chapter 1. Introduction

Harness the serenity of a calm mind to power your productivity with "Peaceful Productivity: Mindful Time Management Strategies"! This special report helps you explore the symbiosis between inner tranquility and your efficiency at work. Discover a flavorful mix of mindful exercises, time management tactics, and stress busters - all geared towards propelling you into an existence where work becomes not just a means to an end, but a work of art in itself. Prepare to be dazzled by the transformation you'll go through, from being a harried worker bee to a zen master of productivity. Get ready to achieve more, while doing less. Whether you're a bustling executive, a creative freelancer, or a busy homemaker, this report is for anyone who wishes to turn productivity into a peaceful, rewarding journey. Embrace the bliss of balance, get your copy today!

Chapter 2. Unlocking the Power of Mindful Living

Achieving a state of mindful living involves waking up from the autopilot mode we often find ourselves in and observing life as it unfolds, moment by moment. This attitude takes us from a reactive state of living to a proactive one - a place where peace, self-awareness, and productivity blossom.

2.1. Understanding Mindfulness

Before diving into the ways of incorporating mindfulness into daily living, it's pivotal to understand what mindfulness actually is. Mindfulness is a state of active, open attention to the present moment. When you're mindful, you observe your thoughts and feelings without judgment. Instead of letting your life pass you by, mindfulness means living in the moment and awakening to experience.

Despite its simplistic definition, mastering mindfulness is a journey. There's no switch to be flipped or a button to be pushed; instead, it's a constant effort to keep switching your focus back to the current moment, each time your mind begins to stray.

2.2. The Science Behind Mindfulness

Scientifically, mindfulness has shown to have an impact on the brain. A 2011 Harvard study revealed that mindfulness can actually change the structure of your brain: eight weeks of Mindfulness-Based Stress Reduction (MBSR) was found to increase cortical thickness in the hippocampus, which governs learning and memory, and in certain areas of the brain that play roles in emotion regulation and self-referential processing.

2.3. Practice of Mindfulness

The beauty of mindfulness is that it can be practiced anywhere, at any time, and by anyone. You do not need special equipment or a particular skill. Across the globe, people practice mindfulness as a way to add more depth and richness to their everyday lives. Here are a few practices you can start with:

1. **Mindful Breathing**: This could be as simple as noticing the sensation of breath entering and leaving your body. Each time your mind wanders off, guide it back gently and refocus on your breath.

2. **Mindful Eating**: Try using all your senses when eating - look at the colors, feel the textures, smell the aromas, munch slowly to savor the taste.

3. **Mindful Walking**: Each step triggers a cascade of sensations - from the hard or soft touch of ground beneath your feet, to the gentle breeze, to the rhythmic sound of your footfall.

4. **Mindful Listening**: Try to listen to the ambient sounds around you, without judging them as pleasant or unpleasant.

All these require practice, patience, and consistency. Start small, and gradually increase the time dedicated to each practice.

2.4. Benefits of Mindful Living

Living mindfully has numerous benefits which revel in a multiplicity of dimensions - physiological, psychological, emotional, and behavioral. Some of the notable ones include:

1. **Sharper Focus**: Regular mindfulness helps improve the ability to resist distractions, enhances memory and the ability to focus on tasks.

2. **Reduced Stress**: Mindfulness can decrease the levels of the stress

hormone cortisol, thus boosting your immune system and making you less prone to sickness.

3. **Enhanced Creativity**: By clearing mental clutter, mindfulness fosters a fertile ground for innovative ideas to take root.

4. **Improved Emotional Quotient**: Mindfulness helps improve skills like empathy, compassion, and an ability to judge the emotional states of ourselves and others.

5. **Better Relationships**: Enhanced EI (Emotional Intelligence) can lead to stronger, more meaningful relationships both at home and work.

2.5. Mindful Productivity

Now, let's delve into how mindfulness can create magic in the world of productivity.

1. **Better Decision Making**: By helping you stay in the 'here and now,' mindfulness enables thoughtful decisions rather than reactive ones. It provides the distance needed to view a situation objectively and to respond rather than react.

2. **Enhanced Creativity**: Since mindfulness clears the mind's clutter, it makes room for a boost in creativity and innovation, attributes that are pivotal in any working environment.

3. **Improved Focus**: Mindfulness trains your brain to stay focused on one task at a time, thereby eradicating multitasking and the problems related to it.

4. **Managing Work Stress**: Being mindful enables you to handle workplace stress in a better manner. It prevents burnout and makes it easier to deal with work pressures.

5. **Improved Leadership**: Mindful leaders are more compassionate, focused, and effective, creating an environment conducive to productivity and employee satisfaction.

2.6. Conclusion

Unlocking the power of mindful living isn't a feat achieved overnight. It's a journey that requires patience and effort. But, the myriad benefits it brings to your personal and professional life makes the climb worth every step. The secret is to start small and keep the momentum going. Embark on your journey to mindful living today and experience an upsurge in peace, balance, and productivity that you've never felt before.

Chapter 3. Building Blocks of Time Management

Time management sits as the cornerstone of productivity. It's a mosaic in which every piece represents an invaluable moment of our hours, days, weeks, or even years. Recognizing the vitality of every chunk of time, and learning how to utilize them effectively, can significantly amplify productivity while concurrently infusing it with an essence of tranquility.

3.1. Understanding the Concept of Time

Time is the one resource we all have an equal share in. Irrespective of our social, economic, or geographical differences, we each get a non-negotiable 24 hours every day. However, the way we utilize this time makes all the difference. The concept of time is akin to an immense canvas. The colors we choose and the strokes we apply are what shape our unique masterpiece, known as life.

Grasping the essence of time enables us to understand its potential and influence on our lives better. Time is not merely quantitative but also qualitative. Perception of time dictates the value we attach to each given moment. Therefore, understanding its potential to catalyze your personal and professional growth is monumental to effective time management.

3.2. Importance of Time Management

Time management turns chaos into order. It is a vehicle that transports us smoothly from aimless wandering to defined trajectories of purpose and productivity. Proper time management:

- Amplifies productivity as you allocate a specific time frame to each task, thereby reducing downtime, and enhancing efficiency.

- Reduces stress as you articulate a comprehensible timetable, eliminating the burden of overloaded tasks.

- Boosts work-life balance by cultivating a routine that incorporates work tasks and personal time, fostering overall wellbeing.

- Enhances decision-making skills as effective scheduling requires us to assess task importance regularly and prioritize accordingly.

- Fosters discipline and improves self-confidence as consistent adherence to a defined schedule promotes self-belief and control.

3.3. Prioritizing: The Crux of Time Management

Effectively managing time starts with priority setting. Not all tasks are created equal. Various tasks bear different weightages in our lives, depending on their relationship to our personal or professional goals. Thus understanding how to prioritize tasks is critical in time management.

The Eisenhower Matrix can be employed fruitfully for this purpose. Here's how you can construct one:

```
[cols="2,2,4"]
|===
| Urgent | Not Urgent
| Important | Quadrant 1(Crisis, Pressing Problems,
Deadline-Driven Projects) | Quadrant 2(Planning,
Relationship Building, Recreation)
| Not Important | Quadrant 3(Interruptions, Some Calls,
```

```
Mail, Reports, Meetings) | Quadrant 4(Trivia, Busy work,
Time wasters)
|===
```

Quadrant 1 includes critical and time-sensitive tasks. Quadrant 2 holds tasks important to your key goals but lack urgency. Quadrant 3 is the home to things that appear urgent but aren't as critical while Quadrant 4 contains activities that neither contribute to your goals nor demand urgency.

Effective time management requires focusing on tasks from Quadrant 2. Strive to plan and prevent problems from Quadrant 1 while delegating tasks from Quadrant 3 and avoiding Quadrant 4 tasks.

3.4. Creating a Schedule

Schedules translate our intentions and priorities into a strategic time allocation plan. A well-devised schedule breaks down tasks into manageable chunks, abates stress, and increases productivity.

However, schedule creation isn't just about assigning time slots to tasks haphazardly. To create an effective schedule:

1. Enumerate your tasks: List everything needing your attention. Assign each task a deadline and estimated completion time.

2. Prioritize tasks: Use the Eisenhower matrix or any other prioritization method that suits you. Rank tasks according to their urgency and importance.

3. Allocate time slots: Dedicate specific time slots for each task. Remember to leave some wiggle room for unexpected tasks or overruns.

4. Plan breaks: Incorporate short breaks to refresh and rejuvenate. Breaks also help augment concentration levels.

5. Reflect and adjust: Regularly review and adjust your schedule for maximum productivity.

3.5. Integrating Mindfulness into Time Management

Time management isn't exclusively about getting things done; it's also about feeling content, peaceful, and satisfied with the work we do. Integrating mindfulness into time management can lead to a sustained fruitful relationship between personal peace and professional productivity.

Mindfulness can foster heightened awareness of our actions, decisions, and time. It assists in realigning our focus to tasks at hand, reducing distractions, and increasing efficiency.

Some ways to integrate mindfulness into your routine include:

- Begin the day with a mindfulness practice, such as meditation or deep breathing. It helps set an intention for the day, grounding and focusing the mind.

- Practice mindfulness pockets throughout the day. Take a few minutes to focus on your breath, observe your thoughts, or just seat in tranquility. It can serve as a powerful reset button during demanding times.

- Employ mindful techniques during transitions between tasks. Focused breathing, physical stretching, or visualization techniques can help clear the mind, assisting you to fully dive into the next task.

In conclusion, mastering the building blocks of time management can upturn the productivity game for anyone willing to learn and practice. The strategies discussed in this chapter focus not only on practical time management skills but also on integrating mindfulness, making the journey tranquil and rewarding. The goal here is to create a perfect symphony of peaceful productivity, where time brings forth not just results, but also personal and professional satisfaction.

Chapter 4. Techniques for Becoming Present in the Moment

Mindfulness—an age-old practice of bringing one's attention to the here and now—has been broadly recognized for its significant impact on overall cognitive performance, mental health, and—even better—productivity. Before we go into the techniques, let's understand why being present is integral to productivity.

4.1. The Value of Presence in the Context of Productivity

Conscious attentiveness to the present task holds immense potential in shaking up the way we function in our work spheres. It aids in eliminating distractions, fosters creativity, reduces anxiety, and enables us to gain a deeper fulfilment from the work we perform each day. By allowing ourselves to focus entirely on what we're working on in a given moment, we create an environment conducive to enriched productivity. In this tranquility, the task at hand becomes our entire universe, freeing us to execute it with our full potential.

4.2. Reclaiming a Grip on Your Awareness

To deploy presence effectively, we should first recognize the times when our mind tends to drift away. Perhaps during monotonous tasks or long meetings, we just drift off. Increasing self-awareness will help you catch yourself when your mind begins to wander, allowing you to gently bring yourself back to the moment.

4.3. Mindful Breathing

One timeless approach to bolster awareness and presence is the practice of mindful breathing. It serves not only to provide a soothing rhythm to our activities but also to forge a strong anchor to our present moment. To practice this, sit back in a relaxing position, focus on escaping thoughts, and bring your attention back to your breathing rhythm. Gradually, you'll notice your attention drifting less, and your mind will be hauled into "here and now."

4.4. Single-Tasking vs. Multitasking

While juggling multiple tasks may seem a more productive approach, in truth it often leads to stress, errors, and inefficient work. Single-tasking encourages us to invest in one task at a time and commit our entire focus to it—thereby encouraging higher productivity levels.

4.5. Using Reminders

Whether it's digital alerts or simple sticky notes on your desk, reminders can efficiently bring your wandering mind back to the task at hand. They assist you to refocus and regain the ground lost to uncontrolled daydreaming or worry.

4.6. Appreciating the Mundane

Every task, irrespective of its magnitude or relevance, deserves our complete attention. By embracing even the mundane tasks and acknowledging their worth, we can infuse a level of attentiveness that boosts productivity and sets the stage for a peaceful work environment.

4.7. Mindful Breaks

It's essential to treat yourself with regular pauses—another powerful tool to boost your presence. Short breaks taken between tasks can replenish your mental strength. These could be brief strolls, a hot cup of tea, five minutes of silence, or anything that rejuvenates you.

4.8. Using Mindfulness Apps

Cultivating presence can often be easier with the aid of modern technology. Apps such as Headspace, Calm, or Insight Timer provide guided mindfulness exercises to help maintain focus. So, the use of mindfulness apps can be beneficial in keeping us rooted in the present.

4.9. Practice, Practice, Practice

Like any skill, mindfulness takes repetition to master. The more you practice, the more effective these techniques will become. It's about progressively training your brain to focus, with consistency being the key.

In conclusion, incorporating mindfulness into your work life doesn't require drastic changes. It needs a subtle shift in the way we perceive and react to the tasks we perform each day. These techniques promise a journey towards a happier, more peaceful, and naturally more productive you. Tranquil productivity doesn't have to be a fancy term or a complex ideal—it's an attainable reality when we commit to making small but consistent changes in the pledge of living in our present.

Chapter 5. The Art of Prioritizing: A Recipe for Success

Establishing a paradigm of success relies heavily on the strength of one's grasp over their order of priorities. This doesn't mean just setting a checklist for the day and ticking off boxes. Instead, the true art of prioritizing is an exercise in mindful discrimination, where you sift through the swathes of tasks crowding your deck, and sequence them in a way which yields the most efficient and satisfying result.

5.1. Understanding Priorities

We're all subject to 24-hour days. This limited amount of time makes it crucial to identify what truly matters to us and give it precedence. Our priorities can be personal or professional and may vary based on our current circumstances. Nevertheless, identifying them lays the groundwork for successful time management.

The first step towards understanding your priorities is self-awareness. Aligning your tasks with your personal goals and values helps create meaning behind every action you undertake. Whether they are career-advancing tasks or activities dedicated towards personal wellbeing, acknowledging their linkage to your overall objectives is essential.

5.2. The Eisenhower Matrix

Understanding priorities could be chaotic, thus using a tool is advisable. One classic approach is the Eisenhower Matrix or the Urgent-Important Matrix, which groups tasks on the basis of their urgency and importance.

1. An AsciiDoc table

	Urgent	Not Urgent
Important	Do First	Schedule	**Not Important**

Here's a brief look at how to sort tasks within this matrix:

- Do First: These are tasks that are both important and urgent. They require immediate action and align with your long-term goals.

- Schedule: Assign a specific time to these tasks. While they are important, they require no immediate action.

- Delegate: These are tasks that are urgent but not important. They may require immediate action but not necessarily by you.

- Don't Do: The last quadrant is for tasks that are neither urgent nor important.

By organizing our tasks based on this schema, we not only make our load manageable but also ensure we are dedicating our time and energy to tasks which truly align with our goals.

5.3. The ABCDE Method

Another technique used to prioritize tasks is the ABCDE method. This involves classifying tasks from A (most important) to E (least important).

1. An AsciiDoc list

   ◦ 'A' Tasks: High priority tasks that yield significant consequences.

   ◦ 'B' Tasks: Tasks of lesser importance that have mild

consequences.

- 'C' Tasks: Tasks which bring no consequences at all.
- 'D' Tasks: Tasks that should be delegated.
- 'E' Tasks: Tasks that can be eliminated.

This method allows you a clearer view of tasks that help move you closer to your goals, and thus deserve your immediate attention.

5.4. Prioritizing Personal Wellbeing

While professional fulfillment contributes significantly to our satisfaction, personal wellbeing should not be sidelined. Make sure to include time for self-care practices, rest, and hobbies in your priority list. This ensures that you're not just productive and successful, but also at peace with yourself and your work.

In order words, the art of prioritizing is not merely a technique but a philosophy that values balance, focus, and self-awareness. Ensure that each task you undertake is more than a to-do list item, but a piece of the jigsaw that completes the picture of your success. This approach, trained through mindful reflection and applied consistently, will gradually transform the way you interact with your tasks, nurturing not just your productivity, but your peace, satisfaction, and overall well-being.

5.5. Review and Adjust

It's important to remember that priorities are not set in stone. They shift as our goals, circumstances, and desires evolve. It is vital, hence, to not just set your priorities but review and adjust them regularly. Keep checking if the tasks still align with your long-term objectives and if not, feel free to shuffle them around. Adopt a flexible rather than a rigid approach towards your priorities to ensure the efficiency of your time management.

5.6. Conclusion

Mastering the art of prioritizing is a journey of optimization and self-discovery. By balancing urgency, importance, and personal wellbeing, you can create a recipe for success - a recipe that will lead you not just towards the completion of tasks, but towards living a life which yields satisfaction, success, and serenity. So internalize these strategies, and begin your journey towards a life of peaceful productivity today.

Chapter 6. From Multitasking to Mindful Single-Tasking

In a world that often glorifies the 'cult of busyness', multitasking has become quite a benchmark of productivity. You might find yourself responding to emails during a team meeting, or brainstorming new ideas while answering client calls. Such activities, even though they might make you feel productive, often lead to sub-optimal results and increased stress. This chapter lays emphasis on making a paradigm shift from multitasking to mindful single-tasking. It will provide you with strategies and insights on how to bring about this change and enhance your productivity through peace.

6.1. Why Shift to Mindful Single-Tasking?

Research has increasingly shown the pitfalls of multitasking. Contrary to popular belief, multitasking can actually reduce productivity by as much as 40%. This happens because our brains are not designed to perform multiple cognitively demanding tasks at the same time. In an attempt to multitask, we simply switch between tasks rapidly. Each switch comes with a cognitive cost. This leads to errors, reduces focus, and wastes time.

Mindful single-tasking, on the other hand, refers to the practice of focusing your full attention on a single task, performing it to the best of your ability, and not shifting focus until the task is completed or a designated break time has arrived. This methodology prioritizes quality over quantity and represents an important step towards mindful productivity.

6.2. Benefits of Mindful Single-Tasking

1. **Improved Focus**: When you single-task, you train your mind to focus on one thing at a time, thereby improving your overall focus and attention span.

2. **Less Stress**: Juggling multiple tasks at once can be stressful. By focusing on one task at a time, you reduce underlying anxiety and induce a more relaxed state of mind.

3. **Enhanced Productivity**: By avoiding the cognitive costs associated with switching tasks, you increase your efficiency and deliver higher-quality outputs.

4. **Increased Satisfaction**: You're likely to derive a sense of satisfaction from fully completing a task instead of leaving multiple tasks half done.

6.3. Establishing A Single-Tasking Routine

Implementing mindful single-tasking into your routine requires deliberate practice. Here are few key strategies to get started.

Identify Your Priorities: Start your day by identifying your top priority tasks. This clarity will help keep your focus intact and reduce the temptation to switch tasks.

Block Your Time: Allocate specific time slots for different activities. This technique, known as time-blocking, can help you dedicate undivided attention to one task at a time.

Use Technology Wisely: Use applications that block out distractions and reminders that nudge you back to your primary task. But remember, the goal is to avoid using technology as a crutch - the aim is to strengthen your ability to concentrate.

Take Regular Breaks: Consider implementing techniques such as the Pomodoro Technique or the 52/17 rule which emphasize the need for regular breaks to aid attention restoration.

6.4. Overcoming Challenges to Single-Tasking

Switching from multitasking to single-tasking may initially feel inefficient. You might find it difficult to resist the urge to check emails or answer calls. Here are some tips to overcome these challenges:

Mitigate Distractions: Identify your primary sources of distraction and consciously mitigate them. This could mean turning off notifications, creating a quiet workspace, or telling colleagues about your focus periods.

Cultivate Patience: Changing habits takes time. Be patient with yourself during this transition period and remember that the benefits of single-tasking will become evident over time.

Practice Mindfulness: Cultivate mindfulness habits like deep breathing, meditation, or yoga to enhance your ability to concentrate and resist the impulses that drive multitasking.

In conclusion, the move from multitasking to mindful single-tasking is a journey that reaps multiple benefits, including enhanced focus, productivity, and peace of mind. It's a strategic shift towards efficient work, intelligent resource allocation, and attains rewarding work-life balance. This change may not happen overnight, but as you progress, every step will bring you one step closer to peaceful productivity.

Chapter 7. Befriend Technology for Better Time Management

The modern world intrinsically ties time management and productivity with the intelligent use of technology. When used mindfully, technology can streamline your tasks, declutter your mind, and vastly improve your efficiency. This section outlines how you can befriend technology for better time management.

7.1. Leveraging Time-Management Tools

A variety of digital tools exist today to assist us with our time management objectives. They range from generic calendars and reminders to specialized software designed for meticulous project planning.

A simple digital calendar can organize your day, week, or month. Visualizing your commitments for the day can give you a clear view of how your time is divided, ensuring you are balancing work, rest, and leisure efficiently. Consider Google Calendar or Outlook for this purpose. Besides setting reminders for appointments or deadlines, you can schedule blocks of time for deep work, strategizing, or planning.

To-do list apps like Todoist or Microsoft To-Do allow you to structure your tasks for the day and tick them off as you complete them. This not only gives you a sense of achievement but also provides a visual representation of your progress.

More specialized tools like Asana, Trello, or Monday.com allow you to plan and track your projects and tasks in detail. They support collaboration with team members, setting deadlines, tracking time spent on tasks, and even automating processes.

However, it's essential not to get lost in the myriad tools available. Choose wisely, find what suits you and your needs, and stick to it to prevent your productivity tools from becoming distractions themselves.

7.2. The Power of Automation

Automation, in essence, allows tasks to be completed with little to no human intervention. It reduces the time spent on mindless tasks and frees up resources to focus on more critical, personally satisfying, and intellectually demanding tasks.

In the digital age, you can automate many things: Repetitive emails can be templated in Gmail or Outlook. Data entry and backups can be automated using various software. Digital tools like IFTTT (If This Then That) or Zapier allow integration of different apps to create automatic workflows. For example, you can automatically sync your Google Calendar events to your to-do list or automate social media posts with Buffer.

Keep in mind that automation should simplify your tasks. If it takes you more time to set up and troubleshoot the automation than it would to complete the activity, you should rethink that automation process.

7.3. Mindful Use of Social Media and Digital Devices

While technology can enhance productivity, it's also an unparalleled source of distraction. Be mindful of the potential negative impact social media and digital devices can have on your time and attention.

Constantly checking social media or aimlessly browsing the internet can create digital clutter, much like physical clutter, draining your mental energy and hindering your productivity. Several apps can help you limit your time spent on social media or idle internet browsing. Freedom or StayFocusd are examples of such tools that limit distracting apps or websites.

Notifications can also create disruptions and fragment your concentration. It's good practice to batch check your emails or messages and respond at specific times during the day, instead of reacting to every notification immediately. Configure your devices to quieten distracting notifications.

Using your digital devices mindfully can assist your quest for reduced stress and increased productivity. Applications like Calm, Headspace, or Insight Timer can guide you through regular mindfulness practices, which can serve as tools of decompression in your fast-paced routine.

7.4. The importance of Digital Well-being and Recharging Periods

Remember that, while technology can greatly increase efficiency, it's also essential to periodically unplug from digital devices for mental and emotional well-being. Develop a routine that involves periods without digital devices. You can adopt techniques such as maintaining gadget-free zones in your house, keeping devices away during meals, or having regular digital detox intervals.

Furthermore, it's equally important to embrace periods of rest to recharge your energy levels. Just as your physical body requires sleep to recuperate, your mind needs rest to function optimally. Apps like Headspace offer guided meditations aimed at improving sleep or providing moments of rest throughout the day.

On the whole, befriending technology implies making and managing these tools in a manner that enables us to be efficient and mindful. It involves striking a balance between leveraging technology to improve productivity while ensuring it does not wear us down. When mastered, it can incorporate zen-like productivity into our working lives.

Chapter 8. Effective Breaks: The Secret Ingredient to Productivity

Inner peace and productivity may seem like two disparate concepts. However, just like yin and yang, they are complementary forces that can provide balance and harmony. An often overlooked, yet crucial player in this balance is the effective use of breaks.

The secret to maintaining that tranquil demeanor and reaching your peak performance lies in integrating breaks into your daily work routine in a mindful and strategic manner. You might have faced periods of burnout after long, stressful hours of unbroken work, which is a clear sign that your current work routine can benefit from a few more breaks.

8.1. The Power of Breaks

Why are breaks important, one might ask? Breaks, when correctly implemented, perform as mini reset sessions that help rejuvenate your mind and body. Plus, they can be fashioned to effectively accentuate your productivity and output.

Firstly, breaks help alleviate job-related stress. Overworking without intervals can lead to stress accumulation and eventual burnout. By taking a few moments to relax, you decrease the likelihood of chronic stress that can have long-term physical and mental health repercussions.

Secondly, breaks enhance creative thinking. If you've ever found yourself struggling with a problem, only to return after a break with fresh ideas and solutions, you've experienced this phenomenon. Periods of mental rest aid in loosening your cognitive constraints, allowing the free flow of your creative juices.

Lastly, breaks align with our body's natural rhythm. Similar to sleep cycles, our body goes through ultradian rhythms during waking hours. These are alternating periods of high frequency brain activity followed by lower frequency activity. Essentially, after every 90-120 minutes of focused work, your brain needs an interval to renew its energy.

8.2. Crafting Your Perfect Break

Now that we've delved into the benefits of breaks, it's time to discuss how one can customize their breaks. Your perfect break depends heavily on your personal preferences and the nature of your work. While there's no one-size-fits-all solution, here are some general guidelines.

Short Breaks vs Long Breaks

Contrary to common belief, all breaks are not created equal. Short breaks, often termed as micro-breaks, are those ranging from a few seconds to a few minutes. They include tasks like stretching, taking a quick walk, or simply staring out the window. Micro-breaks are beneficial for those performing highly repetitive work or work involving physical strain.

Long breaks, on the other hand, are generally 20 - 30 minutes long, and are ideal for activities that help you de-stress, including meditation, exercise, reading, or even a quick power nap. These are valuable after completing tasks requiring considerable mental effort.

Physical Breaks vs Mental Breaks

Physical breaks aim to relieve your body from its sedentary posture, improve blood flow, and reduce physical discomfort. These can involve activities like stretching, taking a walk, or performing desk-friendly exercises.

Mental breaks are targeted at refreshing your mind. They usually involve breaking away from cognitively intensive tasks and engaging in low-effort activities like deep breathing, visualizing, or idle doodling.

8.3. Pomodoro Technique: Structured Breaks for Enhanced Productivity

Among many time-management methods, the Pomodoro Technique is a proven and popular strategy that employs breaks to enhance productivity. Developed in the late 1980s, this technique involves working for a set interval, typically 25 minutes, then taking a short 5-minute break. After the completion of four 'Pomodoros', take a longer break of around 15-30 minutes.

The Pomodoro Technique offers several benefits:

1. It infuses regularity to your work and break schedules.
2. The short, focused work windows tout the scarcity principle - limited time stimulates quicker engagement, promoting productivity.
3. Regularly scheduled breaks keep your mental energy from depleting and combat fatigue.

8.4. Mindful Breaks: The Zen Route to Rest and Rejuvenation

Mindfulness practices during breaks can bring a sense of serenity. Mindful practices ensure that your brain gets a beneficial rest.

Mindful breaks can be as simple as breathing exercises, some quiet time, or a short meditation session.

The key to mindful breaks lies in subscribing to the present moment. This practice pulls you away from the cacophony of the bustling workspace (or mind space) and roots you in the tranquillity of the present - providing an efficient mental recess.

In conclusion, fruitful intervals are key to harmonizing inner peace with productivity. Crafting breaks to suit your personal preferences and work requirements could be the secret to transforming a stressful work routine into a peaceful, invigorating journey. Now that you understand the 'how' and 'why' of effective breaks, it's time to embrace them in everyday life and witness the enchanting alterations they bring to your productivity.

Chapter 9. The Power of Regular Reflection in Enhancing Efficiency

Our daily lives involve performing a myriad of tasks, managing workloads, and juggling responsibilities, all with the aim of achieving productivity. However, in this race of getting more done, we often overlook a potent tool that can significantly impact our productivity – regular reflection.

Reflection, when performed deliberately and systematically, can serve as a catalyst for enhancing efficiency and improving productivity. In this chapter, we will delve deep into the power of reflection and how it can be an effective game-changer for your productivity.

9.1. The Concept of Reflection

To comprehend the influentials that reflection holds on efficiency, it is essential first to understand what reflection truly means. Reflection is not merely a retrospective examination of events; it is a conscious, focused exercise of probing into our thoughts, actions, decisions, and their consequences.

Reflection can help us spot patterns, understand our strengths and limitations, honor our achievements, learn from our mistakes, and identify areas for development.

It is equivalent to pressing a 'pause' button in our routinely quick-paced lives. Not to halt our progress, but to review, learn, align, and continue our journey with more conviction and precision than before.

9.2. The Power of Reflection for Productivity

Consider reflection as your personal accountability partner. It keeps you in touch with your actions and deeds, helping you make conscious adjustments and improvements as needed. This continual analysis and adjustment foster the development of highly effective habits that can exponentially enhance your productivity.

9.3. Reflection and Mindfulness

Engaging in regular reflections fosters mindfulness. Mindfulness, in essence, is being present in the moment, fully conscious of one's thoughts, emotions and actions. This heightened awareness helps you focus better, thereby reducing wasted time on distractions or trivial tasks and driving productivity. Reflecting on your day or week can help recognize these distractions and replace them with more productive elements.

9.4. Enhance Problem Solving Skills

Reflection encourages higher-order thinking, fostering critical and analytical faculties to solve problems and make decisions effectively. By critically evaluating our actions and their outcomes, we stimulate cognitive growth and become better problem solvers. With improved problem-solving skills, prevailing and potential obstacles can be overcome more efficiently, enhancing overall productivity.

9.5. Boost Emotional Intelligence

Emotional Intelligence (EI), an under-rated component of productivity, is significantly impacted by reflection. Regular reflections help in identifying and understanding our emotions, making us more self-aware, and aiding better management of our emotions. With higher EI, the collaboration with colleagues and management of stress becomes smoother, thus amplifying productivity.

9.6. Promote Continuous Learning

Reflection is the cornerstone of learning. It is through reflection that learning is solidified, and insights are reaped from experiences. When you take time to reflect on your actions, you essentially learn from your successes and failures, acquire new perspectives, and recognize opportunities for improvement. This ongoing learning process instigates improvement, often leading to an increase in productivity.

9.7. The Art of Reflecting: How to Reflect Effectively

The practice of reflection might seem straightforward. However, when misplaced, it does little more than consume your time. To harness the myriad benefits that reflection offers, adopting an effective approach is essential. This section will guide you on ways to cultivate a productive reflective practice.

1. **Consistency is Key:** Make reflection a regular habit. Dedicate a specific time each day or week to this practice. Consistency is vital as it trains your mind to introspect regularly, eventually becoming an integral part of your routine.

2. **Create a Conducive Environment:** Choose a calm, quiet space for reflection. It should be free from distractions to encourage focus and introspection. The environment helps in grounding yourself in the process and enhances the effectiveness of the reflection.

3. **Journaling:** The practice of keeping a reflection journal can be highly beneficial. Putting thoughts on paper provides clarity and promotes additional exploration. It can aid in tracking patterns and trends over time.

4. **Reflect on Both Success and Failure:** Reflect not only on failures but deliberate on your success too. Understand and honor your achievements, identify what worked, and use these insights to mold your strategies.

5. **Use Guided Reflection Questions:** Having a set of structured, open-ended questions can drive the reflection process. Questions like "What went well today?" or "What could have been done differently?" or "What did I learn?" can give a direction to your thoughts.

6. **Embrace Honesty:** Reflection demands honesty. Be truthful to yourself, even when the truth seems inconvenient. Honesty propels growth and allows you to recognize your faulty patterns and areas that need addressing.

In conclusion, the power of reflection resides in its capacity to provide insights into our activities, strengths, shortcomings, and potentials. Implemented genuinely and systematically, it can illuminate the pathway to improved productivity. By introspecting regularly, we can take control of our lives, our actions, and our productivity, turning into masons building the monuments of our choice instead of just being a brick in the edifice. So, embrace reflection as a critical component of your life, reap its benefits, and transform your version of productivity.

Chapter 10. Managing Stress: A Pathway to Enhanced Productivity

In today's fast-paced world, stress has become an inseparable part of the work environment. Its management emerges as the paramount pathway for improving productivity. However, be mindful, managing stress does not mean eliminating it totally. It is about consciously identifying, understanding, and controlling stress in a manner that enhances productivity. Here, we will walk you through a plethora of methods and techniques to turn stress into your strength.

10.1. Understanding Stress

Before we delve into the strategies of managing stress, it is crucial to understand what stress truly is. Stress signifies any change that you must adjust to, and it is ubiquitous - primarily actuated by both good and bad experiences. In a work context, it is more often caused by the pressures and demands placed upon you.

The impact of stress is two-pronged. In the right doses, it can be beneficial – acting as a potent motivator or a catalyst for change. However, when it becomes chronic and poorly managed, it can negatively influence your productivity and overall work performance. Understanding stress is the first stride towards managing it effectively.

10.2. The Connection between Stress and Productivity

There lies a curvilinear relationship between stress and productivity, often referred to as the Yerkes-Dodson law. As per this law, we perform our best when we are moderately stressed. Too little stress and we lack motivation, too much and we risk burnout.

Thus, the key to peak performance lies in maintaining this optimal level of stress. Once you are aware of your personal stress thresholds, you can begin to build a toolkit to ensure that you stay within these parameters.

10.3. Stress Identification Methods

The first step towards efficient stress management is to identify what triggers stress within you. Start by maintaining a stress diary - a systematic record of episodes of stress. The entries should include the time, date, place, who you were with, what you were doing, how you felt both physically and emotionally, and your response to it.

Over time, patterns become apparent. You will begin to notice common stressors and your default responses. It's essential not to judge or reprimand yourself during this phase. Aim for understanding and observing instead.

10.4. Stress Management Techniques

Once you've identified your stress triggers, you can start incorporating these stress management techniques which can contribute significantly to enhancing your productivity.

1. **Mindfulness and Meditation:** Mindfulness is all about being present in the moment. Meditation is a way of practicing mindfulness. Spending a few minutes in meditation can restore your inner peace. Besides, mindfulness can also aid in preventing stress from escalating by understanding negative thoughts and emotions.

2. **Discerning what can be controlled:** It's imperative to understand that not everything is within our control. Stressing over uncontrollable events only drains your energy. Instead, try to focus on things that you can control like your reactions and responses to situations.

3. **Physical Rejuvenation:** Exercise, sleep, and good nutrition can provide the much-needed energy and mental stamina to deal with stressors. Regular physical activity releases endorphins that can elevate mood and act as natural painkillers. Good nutrition nourishes the body and stabilizes your mood, leading to improved overall wellbeing.

4. **Emotional Catharsis:** Venting your feelings can be a good stress reliever. This could be through journaling, speaking to a friend or a professional, or expressive arts.

5. **Stay Organized:** A cluttered work environment can lead to a cluttered mind. Efficiently managing time, setting goals, and keeping your workspace tidy can go a long way in reducing unnecessary stress.

6. **Enhance emotional intelligence:** Emotional intelligence refers to recognizing, understanding, and managing our own emotions and the emotions of others. By enhancing your emotional intelligence, you can better manage stress, turn conflict into cooperation, and otherwise improve effectiveness while working with others.

By incorporating these techniques into your daily routine, you can equip yourself with the skills necessary to manage stress effectively, which will ultimately enhance your productivity.

10.5. Evaluating and Adjusting Your Stress Management Techniques

As we continue to evolve in our personal and professional lives, so too should our stress management techniques. Routine assessment of your implemented techniques become essential.

Check in with yourself regularly. Has your stress decreased? Has your productivity improved? Are there certain techniques that aren't providing the results you'd hoped? The process of stress management is a continual cycle of implementation, assessment, adjustment, and re-assessment.

To conclude, your ability to manage stress directly influences your productivity. By understanding stress, identifying your triggers, incorporating effective stress management techniques, and continually evaluating their potency, an ideal equilibrium can be established. Stress management then can pave the way for not only enhanced productivity but also a balanced and healthy life.

Chapter 11. Nurturing Habits for a Lifetime of Peaceful Productivity

Mindful habits set the foundation for a lifetime of peaceful productivity. By incorporating certain behaviors into your day-to-day life, you can engineer an atmosphere that favors tranquility and efficiency. These habits don't just reduce stress, they amplify your ability to focus and accomplish tasks.

11.1. Understanding Mindfulness

Mindfulness simply refers to the practice of fully focusing on the present moment with a non-judgmental mindset. It invites you to be aware of your thoughts, emotions, and actions, facilitating you to act consciously rather than react impulsively. It's being "in the zone", immersed wholeheartedly in the task at hand, whether it's writing a report or washing dishes.

So, how does mindfulness contribute to productivity? When we are present, we can discern details we might otherwise overlook, devise ingenious solutions, think more clearly, and execute tasks more efficiently. In essence, being mindful is like shining a beacon on the path to enhanced productivity.

11.2. Turning Mundane into Mindfulness: A Daily Practice

Practicing mindfulness isn't confined to meditating in solitude. Fostering mindfulness can start with routine tasks—activities performed daily—but treated with conscious attentiveness.

Something as simple as savoring your morning coffee, noticing its aroma, its taste, its warmth. This embeds mindfulness into your day, enabling you to replicate it in your tasks.

When you get to work, approach tasks with the same mindfulness. Take a deep breath before kicking off a project, small or big, and visualize its successful completion. Focusing on one task at a time, dedicating your full attention, you'll see an evident increase in efficiency and a reduction in stress or — paradoxically — in perceived busy-ness.

11.3. The Magic of Meditation

Meditation is another potent tool you can use to nurture mindfulness. Set aside at least 15 minutes a day for this practice. Find a peaceful spot, free of distractions. Sit in a comfortable position with your eyes closed. Simply focus on your breath—in and out. When distractions arise, as they inevitably will, gently drift them away by re-centering your focus on your breath.

This process enhances your ability to concentrate, fostering inner peace, refining decision-making skills, and boosting overall productivity. Regular meditation also cuts the roots of stress and anxiety, allowing you to be more resourceful, resilient, and above all—peacefully productive.

11.4. Establishing Digital Boundaries

In today's interconnected world, it's virtually impossible to escape from the digital realm. While technology can enhance productivity, unbounded use contributes to stress, distractions, and reduced efficiency. Practicing digital mindfulness is a non-negotiable facet of peaceful productivity.

Set boundaries on when and where you use your digital devices. Dedicate time slots for checking emails and social media instead of allowing disruptions throughout the day. Use tools and apps that promote focus rather than distract – focus timers, task management tools, and digital mindfulness apps can be pivotal tools.

Using technology mindfully facilitates productivity by ensuring your technologies serve you, not the other way around. This boundary can save you from unnecessary stress and target your energy more efficiently.

11.5. Nourishing Your Body for Peak Performance

Physical well-being is undeniably linked to productivity. A well-nourished, active body fosters a sharp, calm, and productive mind. Incorporate a balanced diet, regular exercise, and adequate sleep into your routine to optimize performance.

A balanced diet fuels the mind and body, increasing energy levels and cognitive functions. Regular exercise like yoga or simply walking releases endorphins, the 'feel-good' hormones that spark joy and refresh the mind. Lastly, adequate sleep rejuvenates the body and mind, resetting them for the next day's tasks. Respect your body's needs by giving it proper nourishment to function at its peak.

11.6. Prioritizing: The Key to Peaceful Efficiency

Prioritizing tasks is the backbone of mindful time management. Instead of racing to accomplish an overwhelming list of vague tasks, smart prioritization provides focus and clarity.

Adopt a productivity method that resonates with you. Techniques like the Eisenhower Box or the 80/20 rule can be effective. Prioritize tasks based on urgency and importance. Recognize that not all tasks deserve your energy. Learn to delegate, delay, or delete tasks that do not align with your priorities.

By prioritizing, you allow yourself to dedicate time and energy to the tasks that truly matter. This brings order to your workflow, thereby reducing stress and triggering a state of peaceful productivity.

11.7. Reflecting and Adjusting

It's crucial to routinely assess how your adopted habits are serving your peaceful productivity. Review your progress regularly and make necessary adjustments. Remember that what works for others might not work for you, and that's okay. Strive to find what strategies truly align with your productivity objectives and life situations. Embrace change and be open to experiment.

In the journey of nurturing habits for a lifetime of peaceful productivity, remember to stay kind to yourself. Establishing new habits take time. Celebrate small victories, and don't beat yourself up over occasional stumbles. After all, the essence of peaceful productivity lies in blending effectiveness with inner tranquility, not perfection.

Remember, the goal is to live and work in a state of relaxed efficiency, making the most of your time without adding stress or overwhelm. Through mindfulness and prioritization, you can transform your work, making your productivity not only peaceful but a truly rewarding experience.